I AM DIFFERENT

JUST LIKE YOU

Small Things Publishing

Globe, Arizona, USA

Text Copyright © 2019 Rebecca DalMolin
Illustrations Copyright © 2019 Megan Speirs Mack
All rights reserved. Neither this book nor any parts within may be sold or reproduced in any form (electronic, mechanical, photocopying, recording, or otherwise) without written consent from the publisher and copyright holders. This book contains referential websites and social media handles. The author/publisher takes no responsibility for the practices of these companies and individuals and/or the performance of any product or service that they may provide.

Editing by Bobbie Hinman
Primary photography by Kathryn Mertz
Illustrations, cover and book design by Megan Speirs Mack
Other photos courtesy of various contributors
are used with permission.

Library of Congress Control Number 2018911312
First Edition
ISBN (Print) 978-1-7326486-0-9

Publisher's Cataloging-in-Publication Data
provided by Five Rainbows Cataloging Services
Names: DalMolin, Rebecca, author. | Mack, Megan Speirs, illustrator. | Mertz, Kathryn, photographer.
Title: I am different just like you! / Rebecca DalMolin ; Megan Speirs Mack, illustrator ; Kathryn Mertz, photographer.
Description: Globe, AZ : Small Things Publishing, 2019. | Summary: A little girl with Down syndrome takes her friend on a journey to learn more about the condition. | Audience: Grades K-5.
Identifiers: LCCN 2018911312 | ISBN 978-1-7326486-0-9 (hardcover)
Subjects: LCSH: Social integration--Juvenile fiction. | Children's stories. | CYAC: Down syndrome--Fiction. | Children with disabilities--Fiction. | Friendship--Fiction. | BISAC: JUVENILE FICTION / Disabilities & Special Needs. | JUVENILE FICTION / Social Themes / Friendship. | JUVENILE FICTION / Girls & Women.
Classification: LCC PZ7.1.D287 Iam 2019 (print) | LCC PZ7.1.D287 (ebook) | DDC [Fic]--dc23.

Printed and Bound in South Korea
03/01/2020
A percentage of sales from this book go to organizations that support the Down syndrome community.

Thomas

Brynlee

Special thanks to parents who contributed photos of their children

Wesley

A big thank you to Dr. Corby-Harris for sharing her knowledge and expertise.

Isaiah

Brynlee

MacKenzie

Corben

Lola

Jordan

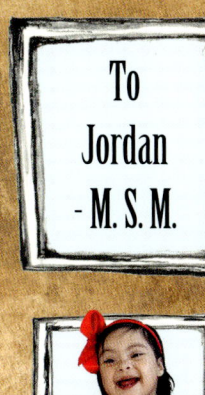
To Jordan
- M. S. M.

Ariel

Terrence

To Mrs. Gaber for igniting my passion for photography
- K. M.

Zoe Ann

To my fellow Rockin' moms and dads and the little ones who connect us
- R. D.

Jeremy

Caleb

Elizabeth

Small things Publishing
www.smallthingspublishing.com
Globe, AZ 85501 USA

Important Message From the Author

Adella is my daughter and I know firsthand how difficult it can be to explain what Down syndrome is, especially to other children. It is my hope that this book will provide its readers with the information necessary to have an open and productive discussion about Down syndrome and an understanding of how to interact with someone who is different than themselves. Despite their differences, all children have one thing in common — the desire to be loved, included and heard.

JUST LIKE YOU!

I AM DIFFERENT JUST LIKE YOU!

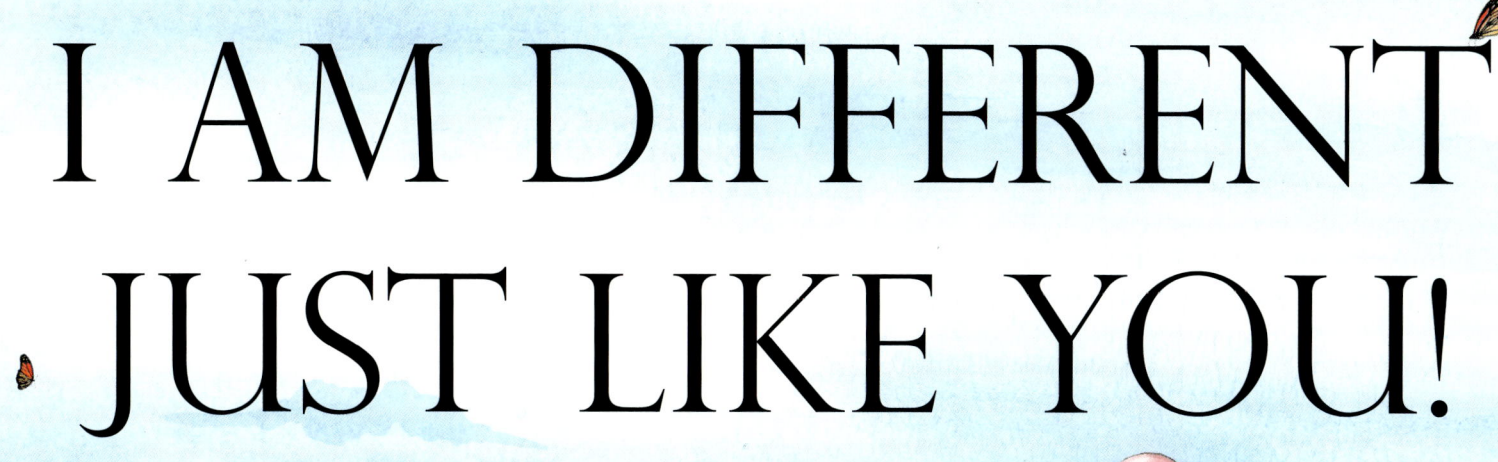

illustrated by
Megan Speirs Mack

Rebecca DalMolin

photography by
Kathryn Mertz

My name is Adella and I have Down syndrome.

foot bones

mouth

kidneys

hand

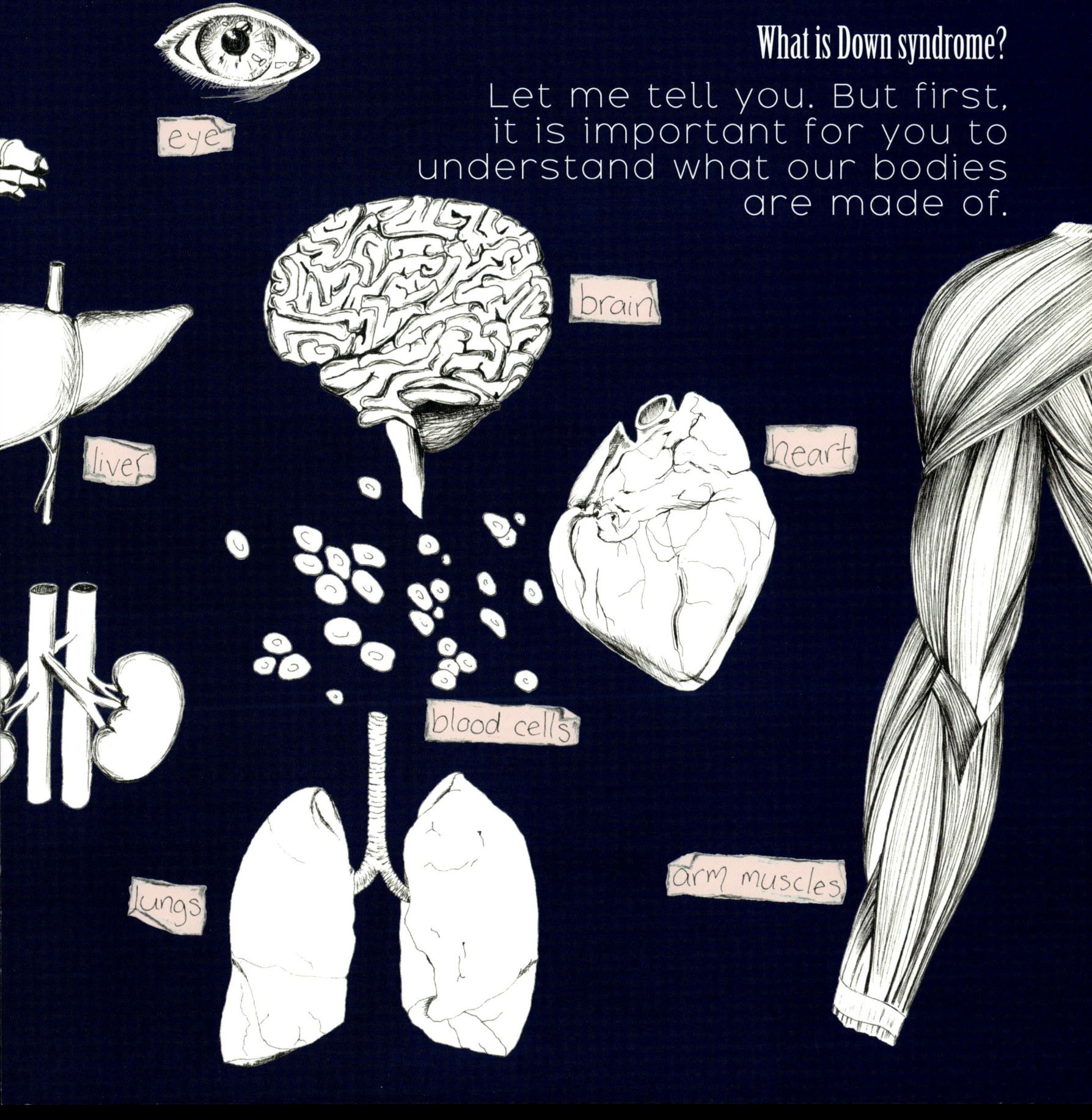

In order
to do that,
we need
to build a
snowman.

Do you know where snowmen come from?
Do they just fall from the sky?
No, that would be silly!
And a little scary.

Snowflakes – NOT SNOWMEN – fall from the sky!
As more and more snowflakes fall, they pile up and stick together.

The best way to make a snowman is to first make a snowball,

then roll it across the snow-covered ground.

As it rolls, more and more snowflakes will stick together and the ball will begin to grow.

Make a few more snowballs,

add some sticks

and rocks,

a hat

and a carrot,

and you now have a snowman.

You will have gone from snowflake...to snowball...to snowman.
So, you see, even though snowflakes are really, really small, if you put a lot of them together, you can build a very, very big snowman.

Just like a snowman, **your body** is made up of very tiny pieces. But instead of snowflakes, your body is made of cells. These cells are so tiny, you can't even see them unless you look at them through a microscope.

8 weeks

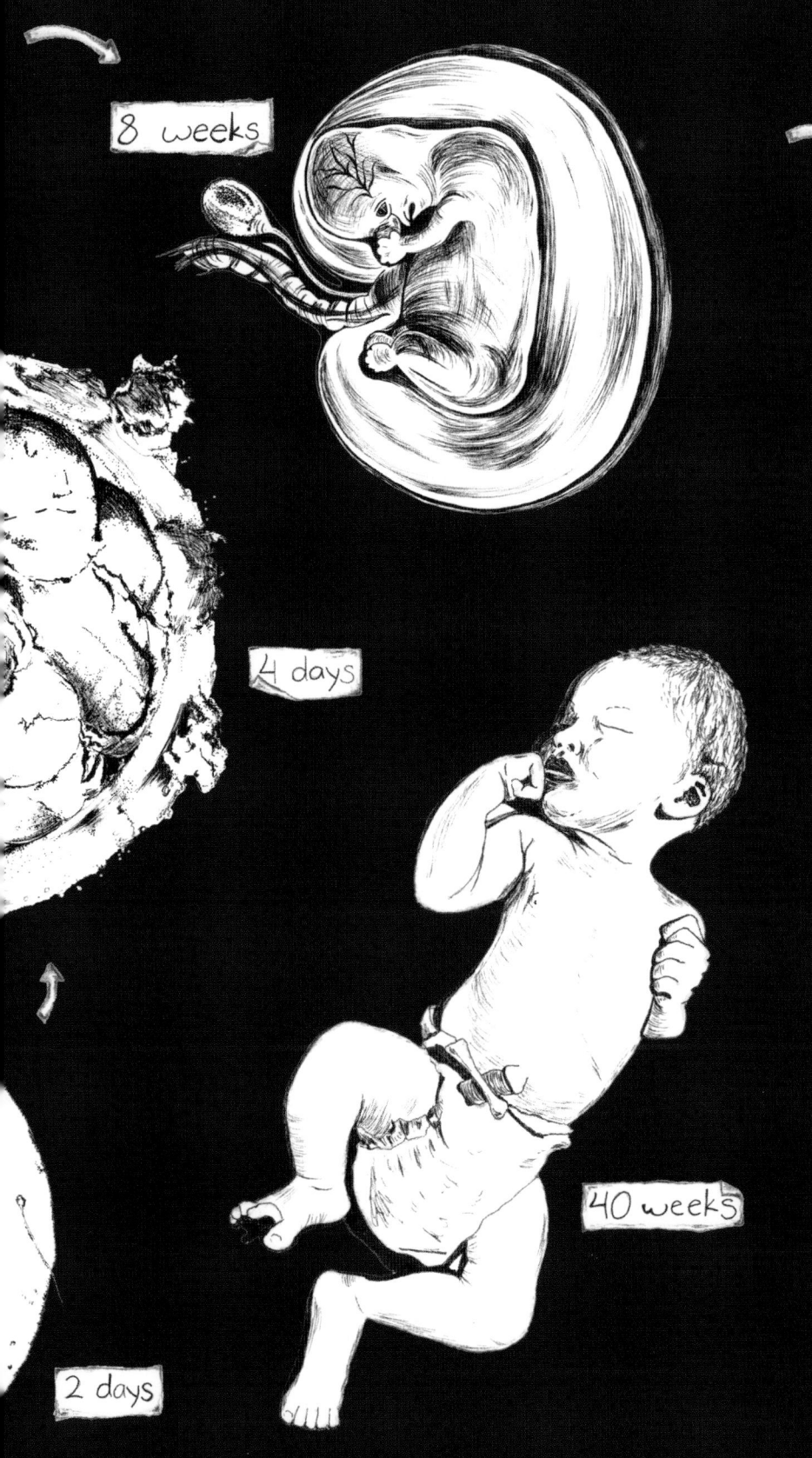

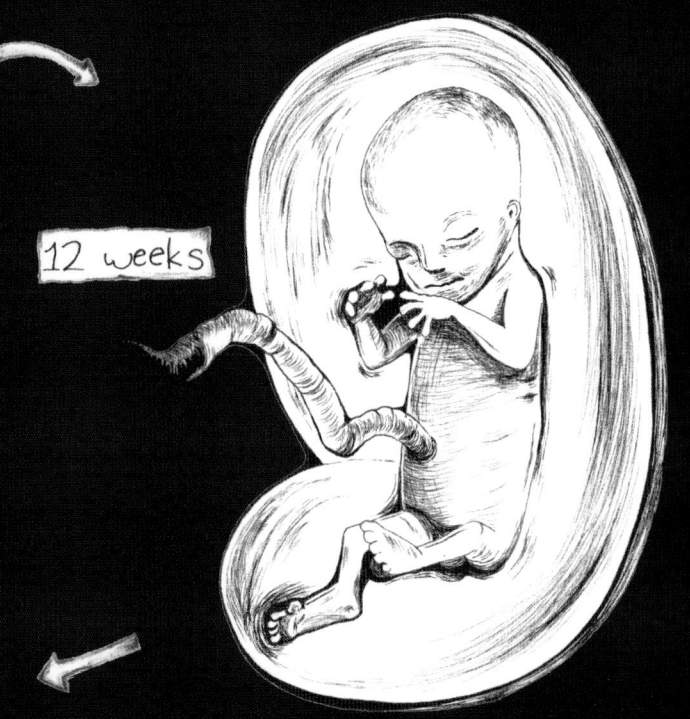

12 weeks

4 days

40 weeks

2 days

Just like the snowman started off as one little snowflake, your body started off as one tiny cell. That cell grew. It divided into two cells. Those two cells grew and divided and became four cells. This went on and on. Soon, just like the snowflake became a snowman, the growing pile of cells became a person — a small, brand-new YOU!

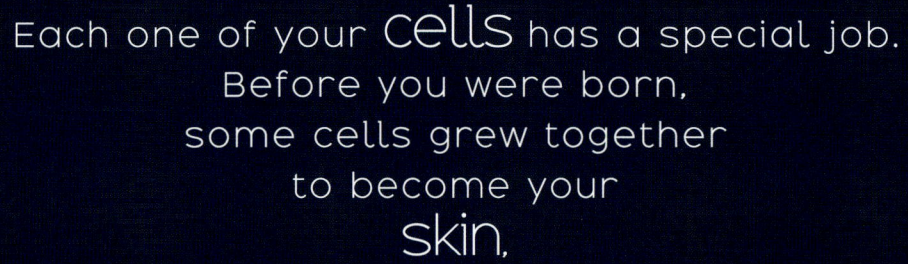

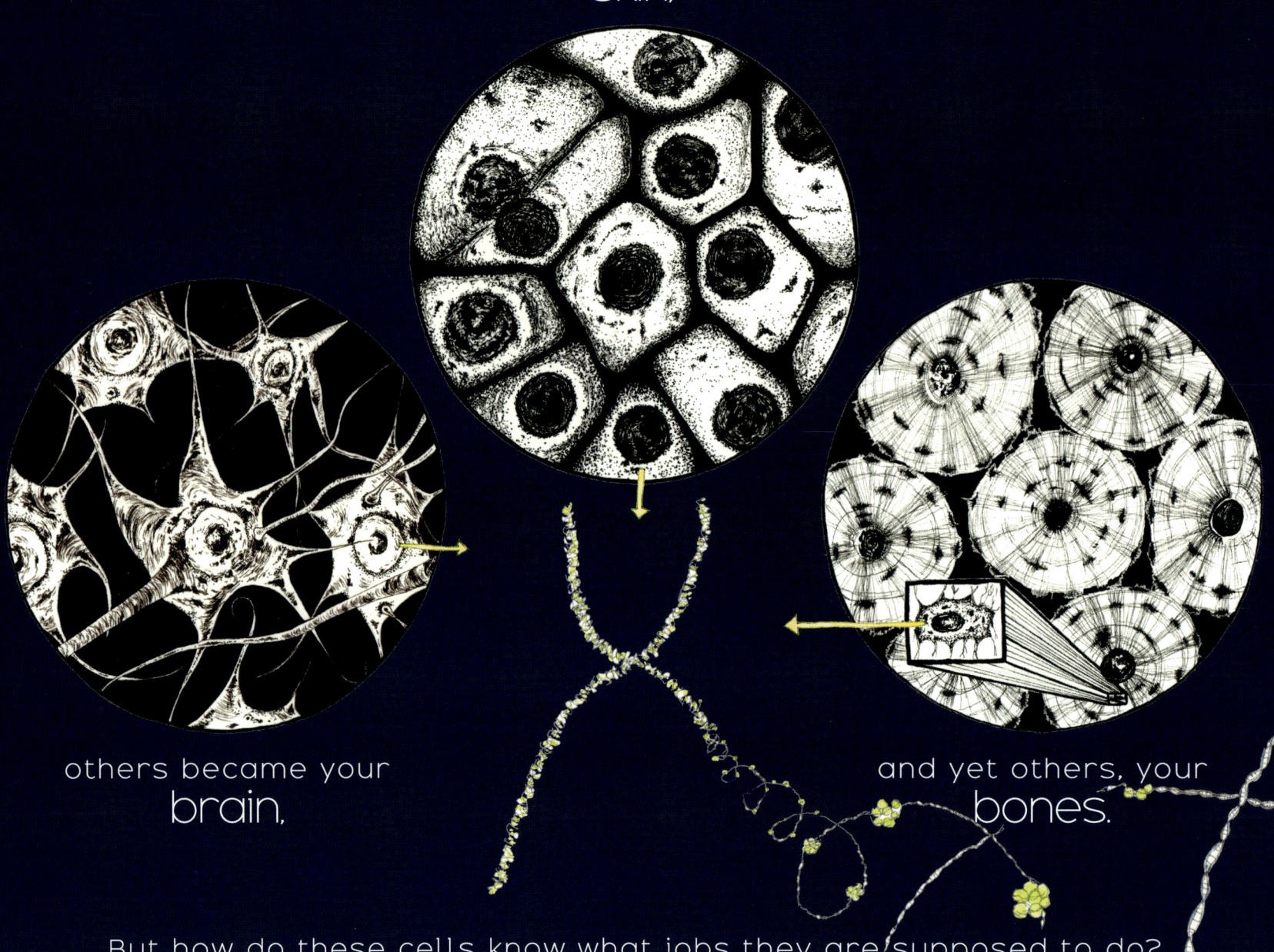

Each one of your cells has a special job.
Before you were born,
some cells grew together
to become your
skin,

others became your
brain,

and yet others, your
bones.

But how do these cells know what jobs they are supposed to do?

The answer is chromosomes.

What are chromosomes?

They are tiny thread-like structures inside each of your cells. They are like your cell's instruction manual. Chromosomes tell the cells **what** they are supposed to do and **how** to do it.

They tell your skin cells whether they should be light or dark. They tell your hair cells whether they should be straight or curly. They tell your eye cells whether they should be blue or green or brown.

A structure is something made up of smaller pieces.

A building is a structure. It is made up of pieces of wood, stone, and metal. Or, sometimes, even blocks.

Chromosomes are very small structures made up of even smaller pieces called DNA.

Did you know? Everyone's DNA is 99.9% the same, but no two people are identical.

Some people, like me, are born with cells

that have an extra chromosome.

That's like having an instruction manual with an extra page — it can be super confusing! This makes it difficult for some of my cells to know exactly what their job is and how to do it.

The Many Ways I Am Just Like You

Sometimes it can be hard for my friends to understand what I'm saying, but I love to talk – just like you!

I may not be as fast as some of my friends,

but I love to run – just like you!

Sometimes I'm scared by LOUD noises and large groups of people,

but I love to play with my friends and family —
just like you!

Hugs always make me feel better — just like you!

Not everything is hard for me to do.
There are some things I'm really good at —
just like you!

I'm really good at singing songs,
making people smile and
taking care of my little sister.

I also love to ride horses, and I'm a very good dancer!

Maybe I'll be a teacher like **Noelia Garella**. She teaches preschool in Argentina!

Maybe I'll own a business like **John Cronin**. He has sold over 120,000 of his crazy socks!

Maybe I'll be an actress like Lauren Potter. She has been in over 50 episodes of the TV show Glee!

Maybe I'll be a Special Olympian like **Melissa Reilly**. She has won gold medals in swimming, skiing and cycling!

Maybe I'll be a mountain climber like **Eli Reimer** and reach the base camp on Mt. Everest!

Maybe I'll be a fashion designer like
Isabella Springmühl.
Her clothes were featured during Fashion Week in London!

So you see, all of these people have Down syndrome, but that doesn't stop them from doing incredible things. Some things are easy for us to do and some things are more difficult. These differences make us unique. So, next time you meet someone who is different from you, just give them a big smile and say,

"You are different — just like me,
and I am different — just like you!"

All About You! What Makes You Different?

I love to talk.

I don't run very fast.

What is something YOU love to do?

Is there something that's hard for YOU to do?

A Special Thank You to Our Role Models

Madeline Stuart

Madeline Stuart first began breaking boundaries after becoming the world's first professional model with Down syndrome to star in a brand campaign. She has since walked in numerous fashion shows across the globe, including five seasons as a participant in New York Fashion Week. Madeline has also been featured in leading publications, such as Vogue, Cosmopolitan and The New York Times.

In addition, she has been named by Forbes Magazine as the number one influential person for Diversity in Fashion for her role in "normalizing Down syndrome."

Thank you, Madeline!

www.madelinestuartmodel.com
- @madelinesmodeling_
- @madelinesmodeling
- @Madeline_Stuart
- Madeline Stuart

Noelia Garella

In 2012, Noelia Garella became Argentina's first preschool teacher with Down syndrome. Having overcome an incredible amount of prejudice, she continues to inspire the Down syndrome community and her students with her positivity and perseverance.

Thank you, Noelia!

John Cronin

John Cronin and his father entered the Crazy Sock industry in 2016. Since then, their multimillion-dollar business has shipped over 120,000 orders worldwide, created 39 jobs (18 of which are filled by individuals with disabilities) and generated over $140,000 for various charities. In March 2019, John was named "Entrepreneur of the Year" by the Long Island Chapter of Entrepreneurs' Organization.
Thank you, John!
www.johnscrazysocks.com
@johnscrazysocks

Eli Reimer

In 2013, after 10 days and 70 miles of walking, Eli Reimer became the first American teen with Down syndrome to make it to the Mount Everest base camp in Nepal.
This led to his ultimately raising $85,000 for the Elisha Foundation, which strives to spread awareness and provide spiritual, physical and developmental resources to disabled populations throughout the world.
Thank you, Eli!

Frank Stephens

John Franklin "Frank" Stephens has been an advocate for people with Down syndrome for many years. In 2016, the Global Down Syndrome Foundation awarded him the Quincy Jones Exceptional Advocacy Award. He has subsequently spoken before the U.S. Congress and the United Nations on behalf of the Down syndrome community.

Thank you, Frank!

f @JohnFranklinStephens

Melissa Reilly

In 2010, Melissa Reilly was inducted into the Special Olympics Massachusetts Hall of Fame. Four years later, she received the Samantha Marcia Stevens Award for her "excellence in raising positive awareness for the skills and strengths of people with Down syndrome and other intellectual disabilities." She currently works as Office Aide for Massachusetts State House Representative Jamie Eldridge and most recently won an additional two gold medals in skiing during the 2019 Massachusetts Special Olympics.

Thank you, Melissa!

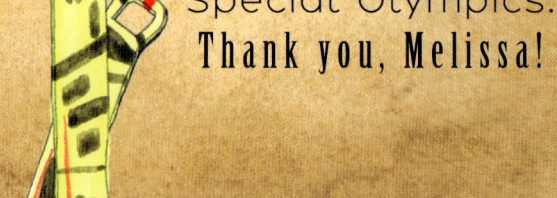

Lauren Potter

Lauren Potter is an actress and producer, best known for her roles in Glee (2009) and Guest Room (2015). She also serves as a representative and ambassador for several organizations, including Best Buddies International, the Down Syndrome Association, the American Association of People with Disabilities and the Special Olympics.
Thank you, Lauren!
@thelaurenpotter

Isabella Springmühl

Isabella Springmühl's fashion designs have been showcased throughout the world. In 2016, she became the first fashion designer with Down syndrome to participate in London Fashion Week. She currently has her own clothing line and online boutique, which include clothes designed specifically for people with Down syndrome.
Thank you, Isabella!
www.animazul.com/collections/down2xjabelle
@downtoxjabelle_
@DowntoXjabelle

Assisting Children in Understanding Down Syndrome

As you read this book to your children or students, keep in mind that *you* have the ability to set the tone for how people with disabilities are treated. If you set an example of patience, inclusion and acceptance, your children or students will follow. Always encourage positive and appropriate language when discussing people with Down syndrome.

It is okay to look and notice differences in others. Let children know that it is okay to ask questions. I appreciate it when Adella and I have the opportunity to teach others what we have learned from our own experiences, and perhaps open their minds and hearts to the beauty they will find in people with Down syndrome.

It is also important to remember that people with Down syndrome can understand more than they can communicate, and that includes negative and derogatory language, such as the r-word. Encourage your children and students to stop using unkind words, while being mindful of the language you use yourself.

(Spread the word to end the word. www.r-word.org)

While discussing this book with children, there will likely be some who do not understand the science behind Down syndrome. That's okay. The main objective of this book is not to teach genetics. Its purpose is to provide a safe and positive setting in which to discuss how important and special our differences can be. This book will give children the tools to be able to more easily relate to other children who, at first glance, appear to be very different from themselves.

When Adella was about six months old, we met an elderly woman in the grocery store. She looked as though she hadn't smiled in decades. As we walked past her, she glanced at my Adella, who, in her true nature, smiled and just beamed at this angry-looking woman. To my surprise, the woman's rigid, angry frown began to melt away and she smiled – a big beautiful smile! As I watched with pride and amazement, I couldn't help looking at Adella and wondering, "How did she do that?"

It has been a number of years since that day, but Adella has continued to spread her love to countless numbers of people. She has an ability that is hard to describe and impossible to duplicate. Our lives are more beautiful because of her.

I realize that interacting and working with a child that does not communicate clearly, or in the same way you do, can be difficult and frustrating. But it is important to also realize how difficult and frustrating it can be for the child who struggles to be understood and heard. You will find that allowing these children extra time to process, communicate their thoughts, and work through tasks will make a big difference in understanding each other.

For Parents and Teachers

Understanding Down Syndrome

People often ask me what Down syndrome is and what it means for my daughter. This is difficult to answer because Down syndrome can present itself within a broad range of challenges and abilities.

Down syndrome is not a disease, nor is it contagious. It is a chromosomal condition that occurs before conception. Each of us has two copies of 23 chromosomes, one copy from our mother and one copy from our father, for a total of 46 chromosomes. Down syndrome occurs when a third copy, whole or partial, of the 21st chromosome is created during cell division. Because of this, Down syndrome is also known as Trisomy 21. A child can receive an extra copy from either parent.

Chromosomes are your cells' instruction manual. They are made up of DNA, the building blocks of life and the source of your body's ability to develop and function. Having an extra chromosome makes it difficult for the body to work as efficiently as it would otherwise.

For some children with Down syndrome, these challenges are severe. These children may be non-verbal, have difficulty learning gross motor skills (crawling, walking, etc.) or have significant health issues, including heart defects, immune deficiencies, or gastrointestinal disorders. Other children exhibit far less severe side effects and are able to function and develop at a relatively typical rate.

Having a child with Down syndrome has taught me many things. Most importantly, it has taught me that it doesn't matter where a child is in their development and it doesn't matter how long it takes them to reach the next milestone. The important thing is to provide every means of support, giving them the opportunity to work for, and reach, each new level of achievement.

It is important to note that this is one child's story. Every child with Down syndrome is unique, with their own individual challenges and strengths. Despite their differences, all children have one thing in common — the desire to be included and heard.

Just like you!